Granny Said

"DON'T LIE"

a book of poetry

Timothy Edward Poulsen

National Library of Australia Cataloguing-in-Publication entry

Creator: Poulsen, Timothy, author

Title: Granny said "Don't Lie": a book of poetry/Timothy Poulsen

ISBN: 9780994413307 (paperback)

ISBN: 9780994413314 (ebook)

ISBN: 9780994413321 (hardcover)

Subjects: Life--Poetry

      Australian poetry

Dewey Number: A821.4

Table of Contents

CHAPTER THREE

REALITY, DREAMS AND
A TWIST OF FANTASY | 81

CHAPTER FOUR

EMOTIONS, FROM
DEEP WITHIN A MAN | 125

Foreword

Insights:

Poetry can be as vast as the oceans. It can take us beyond the obvious into myriad imaginings and mysteries. It can state the obvious and enunciate the unfathomable.

When I first heard the poetry of Tim Poulsen, I was at first, amused. It was funny, close to home and family, and spoke of the larrikin I had known since he was born. If you had asked me if the young Tim Poulsen would ever have written poetry and published it, I would have quickly dismissed the notion within a wink. If you could have suggested that this same kid, could have become a philosopher, bush commentator, theologian and humorist, again, I would have shaken my head with a dismissive blank.

For decades I had been preaching a message about the great surprises of life; about people finding their full potential; of growth from brokenness to wholeness. Similarly, I have tried to live as one who was on a pilgrimage from my own dark places to a realm of health and spiritual empowerment. I never would have thought that my young nephew would have been one who actually walked that walk, whilst I talked the talk. Yet here in these poems – of differing styles and subject matter – lies the personal testimony of one who has indeed walked the walk.

As a boy, Tim knew tall sugar cane. As a poet, Tim talks of tall trees. As a pilgrim, Tim writes about the tall mountains he has had to climb and the deep, dark valleys between them. He has known them all. Now he is able to express these moments, this struggle and this pilgrimage with an honesty and clarity which is far beyond what I ever imagined him capable of expressing. The mystics of the Middle Ages could write about the 'Dark night of the Soul' and the 'Cloud of Unknowing'. Tim has experienced those, and given us insights into their power, their foreboding and their redemption. But all this is done in a unique Australian format with unmistakeable Australian colour, humour and pathos.

Tim's Grandmother Joyce, 'Granny', was a remarkable woman. She was a giving, vulnerable soul, who simply knew how to love her kids and grandkids in a very special way. I suspect there is a lot of Joyce in Tim. Her impact upon Tim is evident in his tribute to her. It can be summarised in one word. Love. Tim has found Love and his poems give us broad insights into the complexity, genuineness and unconditional nature of that Love which Tim has discovered as it reaches the eternal and divine.

As one who has been privileged, in some special way, to be a part of Tim's pilgrimage, it is an honour to be asked to write this Foreword. In reading these works, I have re-entered Tim's journey and had my eyes opened to the insights Tim has gleaned into his beloved country, humanity, deep spiritually and most of all, himself. It is my hope that you will embrace this pilgrimage also and be heartened at its honesty, joy and fun at the things Tim has learned from his Granny and since.

Father Stephen Redhead

July 2015

Acknowledgment

From my soul gratitude goes out
To the amazing universe,
I am so proud to be alive in it
And reside on our loving planet Earth.

To the great creator of all life
I thank you for the gift I've been given,
And the path on which I walk
To fulfil the destiny I am living.

From deep within my heart
To my dear family, I express loving gratitude,
Each of you are held in a special place
Where peace and happiness is just true.

To all the beautiful people, friends and foe
That into my presence have came,
Just know, I embrace each of you dearly
And find joy in each moment you all have brang.

With a purpose for meeting each single being
Every encounter teaching something new,
Every one, as important as the next
So for the experiences I must say thank you.

All involved in life in their own unique way
You know exactly who you are,
I appreciate all that has ever been done
In divine order, our journey will continue far.

To the Great Spirit that inspires me to write
And allowed this book to come into the world,
Along with the team of support on the way
A massive thank you goes out loud.

And for life itself as it journeys on
For many more fruitful adventures I do pray,
Wishing that every human is blessed
I wake to give Thanks every day.

Chapter One

The Earth, Universe and Mysteries

Blessed we are as Humans
To live and breathe freely
In a universe perfectly created
By someone who loves us dearly

Let My Words Live

Picking up the pen, peacefully in my home I sit,
Contemplating my journey on this Earth,
Situated in nature, grounded to the source,
I wonder through various moments from birth.

Allowing thoughts to come I look out the window,
Breathing in the energy from the views outside,
So peaceful is the forest standing still and surrendered,
Fulfilling its purpose, it is alive with pride.

Looking deeper, I notice what's perceived as death,
As I see a tree on the ground, helplessly decomposing,
Bringing a realisation forward to consider life,
And the reality of these words that require exposing.

So short a time we have here on the Earth,
Then like all that into this world has came,
One way or another, overtime into dust we'll turn,
Leaving behind two dates, a dash and a name.

This realisation shows the similarities we all share,
From the unknown we all came, back to it we all go,
Everything is connected, though many don't feel it,
Now is the time to open your mind and let life flow.

Walk the walk laid out before your feet,
Know with open eyes, what is there right in front,
Speak truth from the heart and understand compassion,
Our poor race is dying in a dysfunctional hunt.

Give our Earth a chance to repair from the destruction,
As a product of our environment, just stop and feel,
See the pain that has been created by self,
Then go deeper inside to let wounds heal.

Escape denial and discover how intricate you are,
We are all so special to live and breathe right here,
Let your music play from inside, before it's too late,
And most of all learn to forgive without fear.

Once forgiveness is found a space will open,
Fill it with love and let the imagination be free,
Go beyond form and identity to fulfil your dreams,
Believe there are no limits, when yourself you be.

Gripping the pen tighter I stop, taking a breath,
I know I am blessed, my true self has been found,
As a part of this amazing universe, connected I live,
Wanting to give back, I am on a journey homeward bound.

From the day we are conceived the journey begins,
Created perfectly to experience life to the highest degree,
Yes, there are pitfalls, these are all here serving a purpose,
It's here you learn to embrace the moment, to clearly see.

All that happens does with reason, sometimes unknown,
These are the times internal growth will manifest inside,
Then looking through the pain, the climb up begins,
With the higher good being served, it's now time to stride.

Knowing all that I feel, flowing free, resonates truth,
At the tree decomposing I continue to stare,
Having served its purpose here on this planet,
I write in this moment as it gives this message to share.

We are all born good, with music that plays inside,
Before it's too late whatever the music – to it dance,
Strip back the layers from the conditioning of the past,
Walk forward on the path, come make your stance.

All will unfold in order, find faith in the divine,
Let life flow through you, we are all connected as one,
Look at the bigger picture, our time here is very short,
Eventually in time, all will die – Yes, even the sun.

Nothing is permanent, there's only this moment, now,
What more of a precious gift, than life, could one give,
Step back into nature to reconnect to the source,
Find love in your heart, and please let these very words live.

Flourish

The wind blows through the forest
Like a breath it comes and goes,
Leaves break from trees
To the ground, they trickle slow.

Butterflies flutter freely
Birds fly, happily chirping,
Friendships grow from seeds
New life, now, is birthing.

Sprouting shoots of stillness
Thrive in shining light,
Producing a perfect picture
Colour, everywhere in sight.

Watching seasons pass
All creations are glorified,
Every single little flower
Awakens deep inside.

Right from their very roots
Planted in the Earth's crust,
Life is given, water feeds
The love of God we must trust.

So in the time we have here
In light, flourish like the flowers,
And humble the human spirit
For this precious time...
It is ours.

Day Dreaming

Day dreaming about Earth
A planet, our provider,
Between it, the moon and sun
Space is the divider.

Same as with the stars
That hide during the day,
Out there in the unknown
In the galaxy they lay.

What else is out there?
Not another Earth,
Surely to other life
God would have given birth.

We are so lucky
There's nothing more we need,
Within the depths of dirt
Resources grow from seed.

If it's there humans take it
How long will it all last?
In the bigger picture
It's running out very fast.

In future generations
If Earth survives that long,
They will learn from the mistakes
This dysfunction has done wrong.

We are destroying our planet
Or is this how it's meant to be?
Is the Earth going to die?
In my time, this, will I see?

I really hope I don't
But these times are rather tough,
And when the Earth yells out
"Enough", enough will be enough.

Shooting Star

This life, it brings happiness
You know when all is right,
Thank God I wished on that star
For it was shooting rather bright.

I was lucky that I saw it
So it was meant for me,
More than a coincidence
How many can there be?

So often it seems to happen
To guide us on our way,
Like when you turn on the radio
And your favourite song starts to play.

At that very moment
You grab life within your hands,
To breathe in the Great Spirit
Feeling the freedom of the land.

It brings the world together
Strangers are messengers in disguise,
Listen to the words they say
While looking into their eyes.

That person at that time
You are meant to meet,
Always be cautious though
Dangerous characters walk the street.

They wrongly express emotions
But all are good, deep inside,
To them you may be an angel
With wings white, opened wide.

The world's workings are very strange
Help! It can go either way,
The more we give each other
The more peace will come to stay.

And with peace comes surrender
In which you will awaken,
To see all the humans flourish
Into consciousness you will be taken.

Here there are no limits
Boundaries are far beyond,
All effects of negativity
Are washed away with a wand.

The magic of the spirit
Is so great, it controls,
To be spread when understood
Across the wide world, whole.

So look inside yourself, deep,
Know exactly who you are,
And when you gaze into the universe
You just might see your shooting star.

Sun Sister

On the moon man has walked
I find it hard to believe,
Staring from where I sit
Amazed my eyes can't leave.

Mounted high in the sky
In our universe it lives,
Being a sister to our sun
To all, night light it gives.

Imagine if it weren't there
The world different it'd be,
Only stars twinkling small
Is all that we would see.

But while it is still there
Crossing the night sky,
I sit back and dwell
About this galaxy, Why?

Enormous is all the space
In where the planets revolve,
Some greater intelligence
Let's this universe evolve.

A solar system is visible
But much of it is not,
Where are the outer boundaries?
It's not possible to see the lot.

So looking at the moon, large,
Filling a small, small space,
My person feels so little
Putting a big smile upon my face.

The unknown I laugh at
Really that's what it is,
Nobody else on the planet
Knows, if another life form exists.

The Stars

My stars all in a row
For me they have aligned,
Realising the reasons of life
With my eyes I see the sign.

Something so great presents
From a dimension unknown,
Visions seen are seen alive
Vibrating energy in the zone.

I can do anything
So much power's in the court,
Moving forward to success
Learning from what life's taught.

The universe, the provider
Gives me all that I need,
Wants are not necessary
They don't grow from this seed.

Life's purpose is like a vine
Reaching out as it grows,
Winding its way to the top
To receive the light it knows.

To flower at great height
The human consciousness does deserve,
All alive are individuals
Here on Earth, with a purpose to serve.

You may not know yet
Why your life was ever created,
But one day you're guaranteed
To see your day that's dated.

I speak with prior knowledge
For I am experiencing mine,
My time has finally come
On the day the stars align.

Feel the Magic

Feel the magic
Where you reside,
On our Earth
The universe provides.

Beneath starry skies
Our circle evolves,
Mastering life
Issues resolve.

From hard mistakes
Technology thrives,
Into the future
We humans strive.

In a short space
We've come so far,
As gold is poured
Into solid bar.

Resources are raped
By alien machines,
Through telescopes
Our galaxies seen.

Computers now rule
They are a part of life,
Jails become resorts
Keeping crims out of strife.

Boats travel seas
Transporting volumes large,
Bridges are built
Eliminating the barge.

Skyscrapers erect
How high can they go?
Trains steam a track
Many trailers they tow.

Aeroplanes fly
Rockets launched succeed,
Not much else
Do we need.

Nearly all has been done
On our Earth,
So woman go back
To old ways of birth.

With all we now know
Life must return,
The ways of the past
We must relearn.

Technologies to be taken
Back to the day,
Making more magic
Come here and stay.

Now's the chance
The time is near,
A super world can
Come and live here.

An ultimate life
Can be had by all,
Through the magic
It will fall.

In our universe
You must believe,
Then through life
You will receive.

Feel the magic
In the air,
Feel the magic
It is everywhere.

Feel the magic
It lives in you,
Feel the magic
It is true.

Feel the magic
Where you reside,
Feel the magic
As the universe provides.

Little Birdie

My little birdie
Dark grey and white,
Dead on the driveway
What a sad sight.

Picking him up
My eyes cry tears,
Now facing death
One of my fears.

Why did he die?
I don't know,
I guess it was just
His time to go.

I'll never forget
My feathered friend,
Up to heaven
His soul I will send.

The physical remains
Go to the ground,
In his grave
I remember his sound.

Sitting pleasant
At the window he'd sing,
Chirping away
What a cute little thing.

He'd always show up
When times were tough,
He always knew
When I'd had enough.

Living so freely
To me he would fly,
But sadly today
I must say goodbye.

I'll remember his voice
His song I will miss,
Dead in my hands
My little birdie I kiss.

Let Me Know You Heard

On the outskirts of the border
Breathing in the view,
The world's only Jarrah forest
Grows under a clear sky of blue.

From above its green tree tops
Energy vibrates a white light,
Speaking out into the atmosphere
The universe understands her fight.

Through men she is getting beaten
Being cut down and polluted,
To build a massive mine of gold
How much Jarrahs been uprooted?

Feeling for this forest
To her I wish I could speak,
Like the crows that fly inside
Whose chirps echo from their beak.

I only want to tell her
From her energy I feel alive,
But beyond the thought of mind
In my soul I do not thrive.

Here deep within my person
Sickened to sadness I seem to be,
Cruelty caused by greed
Is what I really see.

Projecting outwards my true self
Towards the universe I believe,
Through karma in an instance
My feelings the forest received.

It was as good as talking to her
The sign witnessed, reassures,
That the universe through nature
Mysteriously controls the laws.

Where the Forest Meets the Mine

A forest lives on one side
A mine is made on the other,
Dust thick blows from it
Onto trees tall it comes to smother.

Where is the comparison?
Beauty natural tries to survive,
Next to the impact so negative
That from gold humans thrive.

We soon forget about the forest
Staying focused on life's plan,
Machines eat away Earth's goodness
As the hole in the ground expands.

Mountains man-made are then built
From waste extracted from the pits,
Ore is crushed into smaller pieces
To produce golden little bits.

Companies make big, big money
Creating jobs so people can survive,
The destruction caused to our Earth
In the back of the mind it hides.

Looking at the biggest picture
From our universe, we don't take a lot,
But from Earth our mother planet
We seem to take everything she's got.

Knocking down forests to create wealth
Is positive only to our race,
All those old tall trees do feel it
When their cut down at the base.

Imagine growing for years
To get hacked down to the ground,
Life is over in an instance
By a ringing chainsaw sound.

Then on the edge stands survivors
Living as their brothers burn,
To witness a mine develop
Standing, waiting for their turn.

For the forest who has feelings?
As we are all a part of its death,
Hauling blasted Earth out the pit
No one stops to take a breath.

The damage is depressing
As the mine continues on,
Deep down inside us all
We all know we are doing wrong.

Money drives the cycle
So vicious it's come to be,
In the future generations
Many holes in the ground they'll see.

And the poor old state forests
Well, if they're lucky they may stand,
Anything at all is possible
But who knows when it comes to man.

So looking at the border
Where the forest and mine meet,
Dust blows from the depths
As machines dig to defeat.

So grey and deathly is the colour
This sits next to the forest green,
Raping all the Earth's resources
Man continues being mean.

Gold is the final outcome
Leaving behind a massive hole,
For the forest and our Earth
I send a blessing from my soul.

Earth Whispers

The Earth so quietly
Whispers to me,
In pain it's hurting
As we're destroying its trees.

So beautiful it looks
As a forest unharmed,
But out on the edge
You're awfully alarmed.

Raping the ground
To build world wealth,
The Jarrah is gone
Impacting ill health.

Defenceless is Earth
Who sits there and takes,
From all the machines
That make the mistakes.

Mining the minerals
Only money it's worth,
What's worth more
Money or Earth?

Earth I believe
For it was here first,
Money makes greed
That so many thirst.

Evil's the cycle
That so many live,
For in their return
It's nothing they give.

So as I listen close
To the whispers I hear,
The Earth tells me
It's us humans it fears.

Dry

Clouds dark grey thicken
Dusk fades into the night,
The moon slowly rising
Hides out of sight.

The forest mined starves
Dust dirties the trees,
Suffocating all the Jarrah
Making it hard to breathe.

Roots dig a little deeper
Sucking moisture out,
There's no more water
You hear the forest shout.

Starving for rain
Will these clouds form?
The old forest needs cleansing
So new life can be born.

The outskirts too are dry
Sheep eat down to dirt,
Drought will soon be death
This can really hurt.

In dams low on water
Cattle are getting bogged,
All the gates are open
All the paddocks nearly flogged.

Praying for these clouds
To transform into a storm,
Farmers watch so closely
With hope the rain will form.

Tonight they might be lucky
A long wait, over it may be,
For the sake of dying life
Please come and rain on me.

2011 Queensland Flood

I can't believe this is real
Unfortunately so real,
Waters have risen above high
So the Earth may hide to heal.

Cleansing our land
As humans brave we fight,
Mother Nature, at her best
Oh! What a sight.

From the north to the south
The west to the east,
Flood waters raging
Become a savage beast.

Wildly rising higher
Every minute, every day,
When will all this water
Find a place to wash away.

It has taken children young
Sweeping them to their death,
And don't forget the elders
Who drowning, took their last breath.

It's a tragedy, a disaster
No one deserves to die,
Or lose their precious homes
From an element rising high.

On roof tops people stood
For help they did hope,
Others walked through rapids
Holding onto a piece of rope.

Emergency services came rushing
Strangers became your friend,
All reaching out to help
Many hands came to lend.

Choppers picked up people
To safety they were taken,
From a terrible dream that's real
Traumatised they would awaken.

Being evacuated to shelters
When would they return?
What would be left?
Only their life, they would learn.

Peaking rivers vastly flowed
Breaking banks as it came,
Towns and cities were destroyed
It was a crying shame.

With every drop that fell
A thousand tears were cried,
And the news only saddened
When announced more had died.

From the rescues to the clean-up
Many people were involved,
Mother Nature, our Earth
Surely had evolved.

It was a natural disaster
That nobody could control,
To all those affected people
Out goes my heart and soul.

As a State known for strength
A battle it had to fight,
With the country's support
Through commodity shone a light.

Queensland will rebuild
Grieving deep within its pain,
No bloody Queenslander
Will forget this year's rain.

Forest of Freedom

When the clock strikes twelve on a moonlit night
A new day begins,
In this hour, an unconscious mind
Dreams of angel wings,
Then the eyes awake, to widen
And watch the morning phase,
Drawn to the trees, through lightened darkness
Seems to be my gaze.

The dew on the grass then finally drips
And falls upon the ground,
Now awake, a conscious mind knows
The forest is about to sound,
Silently loud, it starts to echo
Then forever, it is ringing slow,
With the sun rising over the mountains
Shadows start to show.

When the cattle walk to the water
Is when a horse is caught,
Thoughts think back to remember
The knowledge, my Father taught,
Through the hills twists a creek
That flows fresh after the rain,
But when there is a drought
On a stockman's face you'll see pain.

When the clock strikes twelve on a sun shining day
The sweat will really pour,
In this hour freedoms felt
As the forest it seems to roar,
With boots in irons and hands on reins
The dam is up ahead,
And without a doubt the cattle are there
Just like the old fella said.

Now the sun has started to fall and
The mountain tops are glistening red,
The holding paddocks' gate is closed
To count the number of head,
Behind the bellowing cattle
You hear the forest dying into the night,
Then through the treetops the evening star appears
Happily shining bright.

At last the fire is burning
My eyes stare into the flames,
Realising that to survive this life
Your land, you have to claim,
Out here in the forest gazing
At the Southern Cross I feel best,
But now on the Earth
I lay my swag, to have a good night's rest.

A true character of the forest,
my Step-Father Jeff with his dog Roly
and my Grandmother Joyce.

Chapter Two

On a Journey with Travel and Adventure

If I had the chance
Beyond the moon I'd go
Out there into space
Without a doubt I'd go

Clear Sunsets
Over Dark Horizons

Surf the wave that will never end,
Call the road my home, my friend,
Leave the cities' surrounds somewhere,
To return someday when I don't care.

With youth inside creating life,
A positive motive steers away from strife,
The roads unknown I come to lend,
No care inside where the white line ends.

Seek the views of our far off land,
Pass the locals and raise a hand,
A sight unseen is an unseen sight,
Travel the day and sleep the night.

The eyes close as the road comes to an end,
Write on postcards, stamp, then send,
Watch the day fade into the night,
Shelter in warmth under bright starlight.

A journey begins from the day you're born,
Eyes open at the crack of dawn,
The course chosen has no end,
Ride the wave with a friend.

Dusk approaches time for tea,
Looking up the mind feels free,
Stars fill the sky small but bright,
Imagine life at a greater height.

Tomorrow comes like the day before,
Free and willing to see some more,
Pack up camp to move along,
Choose a disc with our favourite song.

The time has come to have some fun,
Doing only what has to be done,
There's no clock just a moon and sun,
It's clear sunsets over dark horizons.

Gloucester Tree

Not far out of Pemberton
Not far at all,
There stands a tree
About seventy three meters tall.

His name is Gloucester
Yep, Gloucester Tree,
A massive old Karri
As old as could be.

Up his fat trunk
They've nailed in spikes,
So people insane
Can go for a hike.

That's right, if you are game
You can go for a climb,
Where up near the top
A lookout you'll find.

But it's definitely not
For the heart that is faint,
So before you climb
Pray to a Saint.

Few make it up
Others half way,
Some reckon ten meters
Is a bloody long way.

With chicken wire there
For the safety net,
Tourists from overseas
Climb for a bet.

So if you are brave
Unlike me,
Go on have a go
Climb Gloucester Tree.

Valley of the Giants

Travelling in WA's south
Through little country towns,
Following a forest overgrown
Where trees wear the crown.

The smell, smells so fresh
That blows through the car,
Our destination next
Is not all that far.

With time aplenty
The views are taken in,
Admiration feels the beauty
For destruction is a sin.

The energy lives all around
So natural it seems,
Radiated to all living things
Through distorted beams.

Coloured birds fly so freely
Plants flourish nice and bright,
In nature's reserve, natural
What a beautiful sight.

Walpole fastly approaches
A clean country place,
From the local bakery
A pie you must taste.

Locals are true and friendly
As you would expect,
This land they've come to live on
Is treated with respect.

Driving on, through the town
Heading east along the coast,
The Valley of the Giants
Is signed upon a post.

Taking the turn left
The road twists right around,
A forest of old growth
Sure has been found.

Trees stand so tall
Lining the road side,
Who planted this forest?
I ask myself, deep inside.

When did it form
How long has it been here?
Are other questions
That I want to make clear.

Just so amazed
The old forest lives,
Serving its life purpose
More than oxygen it gives.

A habitat for wildlife
Within its trees it provides,
Australian flora and fauna
Down south here survives.

Arriving at the attraction
That brings many from afar,
The fourbies idled down
After its drive along the tar.

In the car park out front
Tourists stand and talk,
About their heightened adventure
On the famous tree-top walk.

Walking past them smiling
Off to the counter we go,
At ten bucks per person
The fee is rather low.

A lovely lady guides us
As there are two walks to do,
So first it is the tree tops
That we will stroll through.

Along a raising platform
The hands tightly grip the rail,
Step by step it heightens
I hope it doesn't fail.

Stopping on the first corner
Some photos, quick, are taken,
Then the next incline starts
Where some people start their shakin.

Reaching the peak slowly
It's high at the top,
Looking down over the edge
It's a sheer forty metre drop.

Standing absolutely still
The platform softly sways,
Up amongst the trees
For a while we come to stay.

Just totally amazed, staring
At the size of the trees,
You really start to realise
How small you must be.

Taking in the sights
From the top it is great,
Karri and Tingles grow
Together they are mates.

Reaching up to the sun
Growing bigger than big,
Their roots beneath the ground
Into Earth continue to dig.

Having to move along
As people come from behind,
Up at this great height
From the trees, we now decline.

Still gripping the rail tight
The bottom's getting near,
Looking up through the trees
The walkway is so clear.

It twists and it turns
All the people look so small,
When put up against
These trees standing tall.

When back at their roots
Two feet are on the ground,
But the journey keeps on going
There's more to be found.

The second stage appears
Which is the famous ground walk,
Back past the kiosk
The path weaves to a fork.

Leading you to the forest
The feel has totally changed,
Crawling now like an ant
So small it feels strange.

The path takes you past
The base of many trees,
With one standing out proud
It's the Grandmother you see.

Definitely she's distinct
So real, will she speak?
It looks like she's breathing
And her eyes are about to tweak.

Happily saying hello
This forest is alive,
The magic's seen around you
As trees old, continue to thrive.

Some have hollow bottoms
In those you can stand,
For a classic photograph
You may be asked by a foreign man.

Gathering his whole family
Within the Tingle's base,
A big, happy, outback smile
Is put on everyone's face.

Capturing the special moment
Friends and family will see,
The upmost enormous size
Of these Western Australian trees.

Moving on towards the end
The path loops back around,
Knowing you've seen it all
It's time to head homeward bound.

Taking time to leave the forest
It seems to suck you back,
Drawn to its vibration
Luckily there's a track.

Not wanting at all to leave
To the Grandmother you say goodbye,
Walking on back past her
Brings a tear to many an eye.

Well sadly it's all come to an end
The ground and tree-top walk,
Back out in the car park
We are now the ones that talk.

Staring back at the old growth forest
More tourists become the client,
How grateful we really are
To be able to walk, The Valley of the Giants.

Ending Isolation

Emotions flow while listening
To the whining of guitars,
When sitting back and steering
From behind the wheel driven bar.

This bar travels routes
That were never to be expected,
Across land from one side to another
This country's well respected.

I'm drawn away with reason
As the mission's been completed,
To stand before a new challenge in life
Not to be defeated.

A rising spirit reaches out
Towards a new sight of ambition,
To the voice inside my head
This time I have listened.

In the past so much has been achieved
I've come a long, long way,
So a new journey in my life
Has just begun today.

To drive into the unknown
Leaving behind tasteful success,
Deep down inside it's far from failure
I know I've passed the test.

If the end of the line is ever found
Curiosity will be cured from what's there,
Though the time it takes to arrive
Is something in the basket of uncare.

At the fork the path is chosen
It's the one that's blindly unseen,
But just like deja vu
It feels like here before I have been.

South Bound

Here I go again
By myself all alone,
Sitting, staring, mining
The world's precious stone.

Wondering really what
The future does hold,
Dust fills the sky
As the wind blows cold.

New surroundings, new people
My life now feels new,
But this chapter again
Looks like deja vu.

Emotionally distorted
Why am I here?
It's only the best
When loved ones are near.

Missing my home life
The one that is real,
Torn apart in two
Can my mind heal?

Sleep deep tonight
Of home I will dream,
Forever it feels like
How long has it been?

To long is to miss
Longing to touch,
A short time away
Is far too much.

Though eyes are clear
And teeth don't grind,
Together we choose
No stress to find.

Understanding each other
Each other we know,
Committed for life
Together we grow.

Making a blessing
Shining a light,
It came from above
From a great height.

Myself I can see
The mirrors my blood,
Bringing up the past
Hatred has flood.

Cruelty exists
The question is why,
Walking away hurt
Today I don't cry.

Toughened to tough
Steel can't compare,
Hot as an iron
Red is the glare.

Wet it with water
From her home the sea,
Tame the king down
In the jungle he's free.

Grounded to Earth
Roaming each day,
Memories young
Continue to stay.

Breaking the chains
The challenge is set,
Hearts thrive striving
It's time to forget.

Craig Hart

On my life-long journey
Writing, trying to be smart,
I met a man, mining
Whose name was Craig Hart.

I consider myself lucky
To become mates with this man,
Someone I could relate to
Tough he did stand.

Like your typical biker
Tattoos covered his skin,
And the hair on his face, grey,
Grew down from his chin.

But through all that armour
A person, real, lived inside,
And there was nothing at all
That he was afraid to hide.

He was a train driver turn truckie
A lifelong miner,
Who in the days when younger
Copped, the occasional shiner.

His stories go way back
Full of rough and tumble,
With the best of the best
A young Harty would rumble.

To lose a hard round
Was a rare result,
Young, lean and mean
He was fit like a colt.

But those days ended
Way before his life,
To be steered correctly
Once meeting his wife.

Being made a man honest
He would still rebel,
Though not in a way
To get locked in a cell.

His way involved bikes
Chromed, loud and fast,
When not steaming the train
His Harley he'd blast.

Holding it full throttle
On the highway he'd cruise,
With every ride, the chance
His licence he'd lose.

Riding for freedom
Of the consequence, no care,
On his face he loved
The feeling of fresh air.

Day in, day out
Fuel he would burn,
To rest his Harley
And give the Kwaka a turn.

So many bikes he owned
All polished bright,
At least they stopped him
From continuing to fight.

With no clubs, no rules
It was just harmless fun,
Which has been encouraged down
To Barney his son.

A father's best mate
His one and own,
Learnt from the best
To break a bone.

Two arms at one time
Put his old man to worry,
But back on that bike
He was in a hurry.

Nothing ever stopped him
Not even his son's pain,
Such a passion he has
He will ride in the rain.

So whenever the chance
When not driving his truck,
He'll be flogging a bike
And trying his luck.

Riding for freedom

Making life great,

This man made of Hart

Is a true mate.

Craig Hart, young lean and mean he was fit like a colt.

Good Tunes

Listening to good tunes
On the radio they play,
Each song brings back memories
From way back in the day.

Touching spots so sensitive
There's no harm to reflect the past,
Till the very day I die
In my mind they will last.

It's not like I'm thinking
Compulsively to be consumed,
Just dwelling on some events
At a time, I thought I was doomed.

Then a genius took over
When the fear was attacked,
A little self confidence
Was all that was lacked.

Having all now that is needed
I look at myself and smile,
On the path of success
To find, it took a while.

Excitement fills my soul
As I go along for the ride,
Creatively, creating
To share, with all my pride.

No other way I would have it
Couldn't change a single day,
All things happen for a reason
So just let the music play.

These songs I keep hearing
Are blessings in disguise,
Someone's watching over me
The spirit, staring with two eyes.

Skydiving

On the way to work walking
I stared into a beautiful blue sky,
Wondering what the feeling would be like
Jumping down from way up high,
Turning my head sideways
With my eyes looking over my shoulder,
I questioned as we marched briskly
Andy, the other devoted soldier.

Bungee jumping and hot air ballooning
He had got a rush from in the past,
And skydiving was definitely on the list
Of sports he'd attempt for a blast,
I too had always wanted
To be able to say I'd dived through the sky,
With our Birthdays one day apart
We thought this is something we must try.

Research was started on the net
And a company round Perth it had to be,
Sticking out from the crowd, looking good
Was the WA Skydiving Academy,
With a deal on offer to capture the evidence
Of this extremely bizarre event,
We both agreed that buying the DVD package
Would be money very well spent.

So a phone call was made
Details were exchanged, and a small deposit paid,
For the 28th of March at 8am
Our tandem jump was officially made,
Having twisted each other's arm
Which didn't take much twisting at all,
We had a few weeks to prepare
For the adrenalin rush and sixty second free fall.

And prepare we did as we marched
To and from work each day,
Knowing this was to be a reward
For the hard work we were doing to earn our pay,
Excitement was expressed from deep inside
As each day it did grow,
Getting geared up we were
When there was only one week left to go.

In this week when thinking too deep
The old nerves would definitely kick in,
But being a challenge of life I strived high
As I knew this challenge I must win,
The question asked is, why you would jump
Out of a perfectly good plane?
Imagine if the chute didn't open
Imagine the death by sudden impact pain.

These thoughts I blocked right out of my head
To build up the courage inside,
A free-fall experience from fourteen thousand feet
The sky I was going to ride,
Knowing if I landed in one piece
That my life was meant to be,
Hoping that death is not near
It is up in a plane I must head so I can see.

So after the many long weeks the wait is over
I awake on March twenty eight,
Having gone back to sleep after the alarm had sounded
I was running late,
The porta cot then wouldn't collapse
It was a terrible start to the day,
And just to top it off the phone rings
It's Andy, who got lost on his way.

Telling Andy to turn at the Premier Hotel in Pinjarra
Would get him back on track,
Like a headless chook I rushed around
To get all the baby's gear loaded in the back,
Leaving Ravenswood Hotel with my foot down hard
I headed to the jumping site,
Andy phones again to inform me that
He's finally found the place alright.

At exactly 8am I drove through the gate
And poked on up to the skydive shed,
Sitting there smiling filling in paperwork
I couldn't miss Andy's bald little head,
Standing to greet me, it didn't take long
For him to start about being late,
Knowing he was fishing for a bite
I went along with him to start a debate.

With us both being fully wired
Our day of fate had finally arrived,
As brothers in arms we knew it wasn't long
Now before we dived,
After filling out our emergency details
In case we unfortunately crashed,
Into our full body jump suits we hopped
Once handing over some of our cash.

All suited up in bright red
Really looking like your typical clown,
We laughed while we were briefed
So we knew what to do on our way down,
Then through a harness we had to stick our limbs
Being the arms and the legs,
The tighter it was pulled
The more Andy's gut stuck out like a keg.

Last but not least the tandem master
Grabbed the most essential part of all,
Obviously it was the parachute
To prevent a most dramatic fall,
With a kiss on my lady's lips
I started to think in my head there was no brain,
So from the old shed with cameras rolling
We headed out to board the plane.

Andy was first in sitting at the opened door
Practicing his exiting style,
Then to be seated in front of his tandem master
To create a massive smile,
Smiling at me, my master said:
"Relax we will exit a totally different way,
It will be somersaults that you perform
When we jump here today."

My eyes lit up with amazement
As somersaults I really wanted to do,
But I didn't know if he was pulling my leg
Or if what he said was true,
I guessed it was just a waiting game
To see what happened up there in the air,
As long as the chute opened when he pulled the cord
I really didn't care.

Getting all boarded in the back
The time had come to leave the ground,
I was glad to have a parachute
When I heard the plane's engine begin to sound,
Roaring like something from the pre-historic days
Was it really going to fly?
Taking off down the run way
Through a window to my lady I waved goodbye.

Picking up speed slowly
The wheels finally lifted up off the grass strip,
With no turning back now
In the air we headed to perform a forward flip,
Adrenalin was pumping
All through the cab, loud, were the laughs and jokes,
Feeling like a bunch of poofters
The way we were sitting was uncomfortable for us blokes.

Right in front and right behind Andy
The tandem masters had no choice but to sit,
Being far from his glory he was
Which is licking and sucking on a Thai lady's tit,
It wasn't long till we reached seven thousand feet
And the old nerves silenced the plane,
Up in the heavens we were heading
Where the good Lord created the rain.

To climb the next seven thousand feet
Forever in a lifetime it seemed to take,
Then as the exit door was opened
My heart let me know that I was awake,
Cold air blew in as a solo jumper
Sat on the edge to say a quiet prayer,
Then out he leapt like a wingless bird
Trying to fly but falling right through the air.

With the solo jumper gone
My turn to dive had finally come around,
I wished Andy the best of luck
And told him I'd see him on the ground,
To the edge crawling I dragged my tandem master
Who was tightly strapped behind,
In such a short time so much stuff started racing
Through my helpless mind.

Sitting there on my knees
Not in my life had I ever felt this way before,
Putting on the goggles it was such a long way down
When looking out the door,
In my head I was silently praying
To be asked by the master if I was good to go,
Taking a deep breath in
I nodded my head and said "yeah righto".

Pulling my head back the master from behind
Then gave me a gentle shove,
Out the exit door we left somersaulting
From way up high in the heavens above,
The first flip I expected
But the second flip I didn't expect at all,
Performing them safely like a banana
We then started to enjoy the free fall.

With adrenalin rushing, arms open wide
And legs kicked up far behind,
At over two hundred kilometers an hour
You could say we were in a fast decline,
The old cheeks were flapping furiously
As the cold air whistled past so loud,
Looking into the video camera
I was smiling to show I was proud.

In sixty seconds which felt like forever
The altitude dropped at an alarming rate,
To feel the chord being pulled to open the chute
Definitely determined my fate,
The heart rate started recovering
When the parachute had filled with air,
From deafening winds to silence
Back to the ground we fell without care.

Taking control of the strings for a while
I talked to my master as we fell,
Knowing it was an adrenalin filled thrill
Which would make a great story to tell,
Pulling hard down on the right string
Made us fall fast, spinning round and round,
Then to give the left one a go until
We were only one thousand feet off the ground.

The master took back the reins
Getting me to put my legs out front to land,
Coming down quickly hitting hard
At Pinjarra I got up to shake my master's hand,
Cameras were still rolling
I told them the feeling was bloody great,
To look up in the sky to see falling
My four-eyed, short-legged, little bald headed mate.

Looking like a monkey strapped in strings
With a parachute hanging high above,
The closer he got you could see by the look on his face
The feeling of flying he loved,
Putting his legs out straight to land
He hit the dust and slid to an enormous cheer,
"Bloody awesome it was" he reckons
"But I'm really glad to be back down here."

Giving thumbs up to the camera
To the very end had come our ride,
Loosening off all the straps of our harness
We were thankfully untied,
Heading to the shed all wired
How could I not notice my lady's smiling face,
Who I wandered over to casually
As the kiss of her lips I wanted to taste.

Being glad to survive the experience
And capture the moment on DVD,
Out of the jump suits we got to see
Andy's bald head free falling on TV,
What a laugh it was seeing those cheeks flapping
While diving through the sky,
And to see him hold those glasses
So he didn't lose the sight of eye.

With his arse still twitching, old Andy
Was all wired from his skydive,
What a great feeling it was that day
You really knew you were alive,
The footage was burned to disc
And handed to us by our masters in a case,
For the last time for a while
A huge thank you was said to them face to face.

Having achieved a goal in life
Skydiving, with a good bloke I call a mate,
Was definitely an adrenalin filled thrill
With a feeling that was more than great,
Leaving the shed for breakfast
We discussed what our next little reward will be,
Mentioning something about high speed Go Karting
I guess it's wait and see.

Preparing for the jump from 14,000 feet, me and my four eyed, short legged, little bald headed mate, Andy Wilkes, a true friend to this very day.

Chapter Three

REALITY, DREAMS AND A TWIST OF FANTASY

To escape reality is to lose the plot
Once the plot is lost
Reality will never return and we will be plotless
How do we know we've escaped though?
At times being plotless is a part of reality
Expand your mind, but avoid escaping reality

Visitor of My Dreams

I lay asleep in the early morning
Eyes closed, mind silent, still,
The body though, so, so alive
Deep subtle breathing, the lungs slowly fill.

Peace permeates all cells of my being
Tranquillity, I've laid down to rest,
Asking in my prayers for a vision
I am visited by a supernatural guest.

Having pictures planted, in my precious mind
Asleep, but consciously aware,
Answers to questions are finally found
As I see my angel, quietly standing there.

Protecting my spirit from the unsacred
Her light, so pure and amazingly gentle,
Her touch, it is like no other
She eases all torment that is dangerously mental.

Seeing her face, beyond beautiful, so real
Heals the soul's deepest wounds and pain,
Arising, creation, another dimension
A path is set, beyond the atmosphere of rain.

Travelling towards a realm in the heavens
She takes my hand, as the journey reaches the unknown,
With no care, no fear, just two hearts
Into eternity we find a place to call our home.

In this place the peace is so peaceful
And the stillness, it is just so still,
Together everything lives as one
In wholeness, dreams and visions are fulfilled.

Forever in a lifetime, it is here I want to be
Alive to the fullest, inside this enchanted scene,
Not wanting to wake, I grip onto the reality of my sleep
For I have now met my angel, the visitor of my dreams.

Angel of Thought

I don't know where she comes from
She simply just does,
Like an angel in my ear
She whispers from above.

Guiding me on this journey
Inspiring me to write,
To her I must hold onto
Gripping tight with all my might.

Never before has she come
So often as she does now,
If I could see her with my eyes
On one knee I would bow.

She is what I see as freedom
The one to get me out,
With all this pen on paper
In time I have no doubt.

I hope she keeps talking
Cos I consider her a friend,
Anytime day or night
My ear she can lend.

Why has she come to me?
Is a question I do ask,
Maybe from the witch of white
On me a spell was cast.

Whatever is the reason
It happened for the right,
Against those devil voices
The angel shines a light.

I don't know where she came from
In my head she's been caught,
Never ever will I release her
It's my angel of thought.

Now

Time, take it away
Appreciate what is
Right here, now
It can't be changed
Move into it, forward
Find the genius
It lives in all
Way, deep within.

It exists
Just like you
Stop, Take a breath
Feel yourself, alive
The blood flows
To all limbs
Circulates free
Intelligence unknown.

Beyond the mind

The higher self

Looks from above

Laughs so loud

Setting the spirit free,

Follow its path

Enlightenment

It can't be explained.

Hungry Man

Under the stars
A man stands at a bin,
Lifting the lid
He searches within.

Poor hands go deep
To find food to survive,
Just like a bee
Going into its hive.

Rustling the rubbish
Disposed from the rich,
Scraps are found
To feed the hungry bitch.

Another man's waste
Is another man's gain,
Daily he searches
To cure hunger pain.

The sights on the streets
Sure do open an eye,
Making one wonder
Where the poor lie.

Who will ever help?
In a world so cruel,
When to think about oneself
Is the golden rule.

A God does exist
But it's out of his control,
As people choose
To dig their own hole.

So as I walk
Amazed by what I see,
I start to realise
I am facing reality.

An Angel

An angel so beautiful
Stands with white soft wings,
Coming down from heaven
A gift from God she brings.

Singing a song of love
So sweet is her voice,
To be taken under a wing
There was simply no better choice.

Being saved into salvation
Peace glistens in the light,
To see many more angels
Flying high above in full flight.

All serve a purpose
To someone they belong,
Listen very closely
And you may hear that lovely song.

It guides you to freedom
With a gentle touch,
These angels sent from heaven
Will be loved, forever, very much.

Like nothing felt before
Are their wings full of feather,
Grown from soft silk skin
That is tough like leather.

Their smile is always present
Never to get upset,
I'll always remember the day
When me and my angel first met.

Giving life, along with hope
She saved and blessed my soul,
Bringing two loves true, together
Together we are whole.

Holder of the Light

Holder of the light
Sacred one, visitor of dreams,
Divine being so beautiful
I feel you here in the timeless,
Your presence lives deep inside
Always here never far,
Healer of my soul
I feel you there.

Opener of doors, giver of sight,
My eyes are washed
Now I can see,
Universal attractions
Force knotting souls,
Swirling spirits twist and bind
Pulling together, tightening closer
Internal, external, eternal.

You are a gift sent from above
An angel of the infinite,
Passing by Earth on a journey
For a short time,
So special, every moment
Not to live again
But knowing as a light holder
You draw many after Earth.

A flame still burns
Bright, forever and ever,
Returning home to the source
From where you came,
That peaceful place
Out there in the unknown
Where angels manifest freedom
In the father's kingdom.

Holder of the light
Sacred one, visitor of dreams
Divine being, so beautiful
I see you there in the timeless
Before the arrival,
Arms wide open
Loving warmth burning bright
I see you there.

Dragon Days

Staring from an aged old tree
Where the wise one is perched,
Flames are destroying human life
By the heat they are scorched.

Down drains made of brick
Civilians run towards the unknown,
As the breath of the evil dragon
Is fired towards their home.

From hidden underground cells
The enemies rise to attack,
Dominating with powerful numbers
Swords are swayed into backs.

Turning to defend their families
The civilians' swords can't be used,
Punished with death first-hand
Into swamps of blood they are abused.

Desperately attempting escape
Now prisoners they grasp for the ceiling,
But the swipe of the dragon's tail
Concludes any of the dealings.

A flag that once flew free
Is now deep in the wings of war,
Starving the soul of peace on land
Turning the rich people into poor.

From far off in the distance
A voice echoes towards the horizon,
Bellowing deeply it is the king
Who in his arms is holding his son.

Bleeding heavily from evil wounds
The next breath will be his last,
Crying for help the king knows
Into heaven the young prince must pass.

From a dangerous field of battle
The king removes the dead remains,
Dragging him to his castle
Along the ground the blood stains.

In the castle of his kingdom
Mourning in grief, royalty sings,
Knowing outside on their doorstep
The bells of war continue to ring.

Being cursed by an evil witch
From a far off foreign land,
Can anybody be so strong?
To sacrifice life by lending a hand.

Locked behind wooden doors
The king is totally scared into fright,
Understanding he is powerless
And that he's losing this fight.

Along with the warriors slaying
The dragon of evil takes control,
Breathing his torturous fire
To burn many an innocent soul.

Then from the wise ones porch
Up in the aged old tree,
In full flight high in the sky
Eagles of many are finally set free.

Bound for attack to bring peace
To the land which does provide,
The monstrous birds head to war
Into the darkened mist they do glide.

Finding their path by the sky
To the fields of horrid death,
Fire and smoke signals the war
As it's breathed from the dragon's breath.

To conquer this evil beast
Intelligent eagles observe the scene,
Circling the ash filled sky
Out of sight of the dragon so mean.

Soaring high above looking down
The time has come to lower to fight,
So a message through nature is sent
For the wise man to shine the light.

With both hands on his staff
The witch's wicked spell is uncursed,
Concentrating wisely from his tree
Magic's created killing a deadly thirst.

Seeing a world of war and torture
Starting to shine again real bright,
The evil warriors along with their dragon
Notice the eagles flying in full flight.

About to swoop with vicious wings
The freedom birds focus ahead,
Approaching the ground they give all
To ensure the enemy is made dead.

Attacking warriors waving their weapons
With their wings and sharpened claws,
Rolling them to their death
Before they could escape through any doors.

The dragon in retreat knows
He can't survive the wise man's light,
And as the eagles behead him
They end this horrible fight.

Victory leads to freedom
And peace appears on the land,
The eagles attend the injured
With the medicine of the wise man.

From the castle servants are sent
By order of the king,
Back to his sacred kingdom
All the civilians they must bring.

Gathering the war-ravaged people
Many are found that hadn't survived,
To be buried and remembered
Of the sad way they had to die.

Understanding the war is over
In a staggering line servants lead the way,
With the eagles carrying the wounded
Across their backs the civilians lay.

Arriving at the king's castle
A royal welcome is received by all,
Glasses are raised in appreciation
Of the poor people that came to fall.

For no reason many sadly died
Due to a witch's evil spell,
But now seeing defence enforced
The wicked bitch can rot in hell.

Telling stories while they are grieving
It is heard during the feast,
About how the eagles killed the dragon
And beheaded the evil beast.

Knowing they didn't stand a chance
Until the eagles finally came,
The ones that somehow survived
Were glad to escape the flame.

The brutality of the attacks
Were heard as many tears weep,
Many swords hurtfully slayed
Into the flesh of bodies deep.

Just outright cruel was the cry
Of the civilians as they heavily drank,
The more beer they consumed
The further in their chairs they sank.

In the castle of the kingdom
Together all the goodness came,
Men, women and the children
From the king were treated the same.

Then the wise man appears for the celebration
Coming down from his tree of old age,
To announce to all the people
The time had come to turn the page.

Peace was felt from deep inside
As he shone the brightest light,
To look to the sky to see the eagles
Flying in harmony to the greatest height.

Peace

Put away your gun
Put away your knife,
It's now time to bring
Some peace into your life.

Stop the slaughter that happens
Right down your street,
Take a deep breath
And feel your heart beat.

I know it pumps blood
Just the same as mine,
But do you witness me
Committing any crime?

No, because in my life
I've learnt to love,
Free and willing
Like a high flying dove.

It's never too late
To change your ways,
C'mon, try and put some colour
Into your days.

Days of black
Can easily fade to white,
It's about time that you looked
And tried to see the light.

Pick your head up
And hold it high,
Take some time to look
At the beautiful blue sky.

Feel the energy flow
On a full moon night,
Face reality
There's no need to fight.

Find someone to express
The way you really feel,
It makes you come alive
It makes you feel real.

Realise the facts
That love was your creator,
Cherish the moments with your mother
Don't ever hate her.

Deceitful lies
Are the root of all hate,
Make truth the water
Flood through the gate,

Release yourself from the evil spirit
That upon you were cast,
God will provide forgiveness
For the sins of the past.

With hands closed
And a knee on the ground pray,
The light's shining bright
So rise to a new day.

Then stand united
As the war comes to cease,
Holding hands as one
To live in world peace.

The Magician

To make things happen
Is the magic of the magician,
Into a new chapter
His life has been wishing.

Many eastern journeys
Have opened eyes up wide,
On the belt of leather
All the notches have been tied.

While sitting in a saddle
On a horse mounted high,
Paths were crossed with humans
Who shed a tear to cry.

Rumours true are cruel and painful
To any of our kind,
How can a young child
Be born into the world blind?

Speechless words dissolve
As they appear upon the tongue,
To bring some hope to this child
In church a prayer is sung.

Can any magic created
Change the reality of any of this?
Imagine not being able to see
The face on that you kiss.

When all tell their stories
A hurtful list will grow,
There's too many old faces
That one has got to know.

So the pages of the past
Are now slowly flipping forward,
With ink stained on paper
You can see where thoughts been poured.

To make things happen
Is the magic of the magician,
In a world that won't change
At times you can only listen.

When one moves closer to their goals
Others stand so still,
Hoping that a God comes down
And warms their coldest chill.

The unfortunate turn of nature
Is something hard to forget,
Then seeds of life are planted
And sown with no regret.

Like water feeding roots
Growing stronger as it thrives,
There's a Greater Spirit
That seems to be alive.

Spreading shade provides protection
From much of the world's hate,
Lost and lonely souls
Are being drawn closer to their fate.

New beginnings are here
And clear right within the sight,
To walk straight into a fear
Is the cure of any fright.

Daunting thoughts are present
But helps one find the way,
There's a mass of colour
Brightening up the day.

As each page turns
And closer ticks the time,
It won't be long till I see her face
Right in front of mine.

Dream, Scream

Miles awake dreaming
A vision in my head,
Not good at all
Loved one is dead.

Hit by a train
Rolling down a track,
Nobody was watching
Watching their back.

In shock jumping
To wake up screaming,
The mind was off
With the fairies dreaming.

Why did this vision
In my sub-consciousness find?
To images of fright
I want to stay blind.

Some say that death
Actually means life,
In a dream state
Acknowledge the knife.

Harm won't be caused
It's there to protect,
Against life wars
Choking the neck.

Every dream comes
From the unknown,
This one created
Deep in the throne.

Sent via a messenger
The spirit could see,
An afterlife character
Who could it be?

Is it a mistake?
That to me they came,
Don't want to sleep
Answers to name.

A nightmare my worst
Is now living inside,
Trying hard to forget
But it won't hide.

The meanings absent
It I must find,
Love one so dear
Is dead in my mind.

I know it's not real
But the vision stays,
Look beside my side
Still, asleep she lays.

Living and breathing
I touch her chest,
Dreaming dreams
I leave her to rest.

Just to see her there
With eyes wide awake,
Cures my dream state
For goodness sake.

But I still wonder
Falling back to sleep,
Who's the creator?
In your mind deep.

Sometimes it's heavenly
Sometimes there's screams,
Sometimes it feels reals
These are my dreams.

Off With the Fairies

Tonight they've come to get me
The fairies have taken me away,
Off to some fantasy land
My mind has gone to play.

Here fairy tales are reality
Sparkling glitter brightly glows,
Magicians play trippy tricks
Entertaining with a show.

Dragons breathe fire raw
To be slayed down by a king,
Goblins munch on mushrooms
Dazed and confused at everything.

Gnomes walk a road
Out of yellow brick it is made,
By old mother hen in the pen
A golden egg is laid.

With the witch's broomstick
Rats chase mice along the floor,
Into a cauldron of boiling water
Ingredients fastly pour.

A beast escapes the dungeon
Using a candle of melting wax,
Eagles circle a castle
Finding scraps to tax.

Angels white hum a tune
Creating this world's peace,
A normal human being
Wonders, when this will all cease.

Tonight they've come to get me
Leading me away by the hand,
Tonight I'm off with the fairies
In a far off fantasy land.

The Making of Man

The making of man was rather cruel,
Cunning and sly just like a fool,
He's mixing the magic to feed a disease,
That lurks in the streets pleading for please.

A recipe of poisonous ingredients he stitches,
Passed on down by broom riding witches,
To this, faces of death, come to rise,
With money in hand to buy the prize.

A laneway waits for the coated man,
Like puddles of rain to get what they can,
These are the weak that fall to his feet,
Consuming amounts creating addiction to beat.

Chemistry boiled and turned by a spool,
Change human brains to that of a mule,
People lie screaming till paramedics came,
Near death experiences were full of pain.

Addicts leave families with only tears to cry,
After stunning their brain for the ultimate high,
The man who makes, he doesn't care,
On he'll bake till no one is there.

Some will cure when they walk the line,
The deeper they dig the more strength they find,
Say goodbye to your favourite friend,
Watch will power grow as you conclude the end.

People are falling to near death,
Their heart is pumping them out of breath,
Who will live to see today?
For the making of man is here to stay.

The Time Has Come to Live My Life

A spell was cast by a witch,
Evil ingredients what a bitch,
The effects will last, people died,
This meant war, no time to hide.

Religious beliefs lead the way,
Innocent people were left to lay,
The world will not be the same,
People insane, play a game.

A spell was cast by a witch,
Enough, too much, tie a hitch,
The whole world is in pain,
Can somebody please explain?

Who was born to start a war?
Somebody with a brainwashed core,
With no good inside, not at all,
Evil power made the towers fall.

The time has come to live my life,

For a war began with a knife,

Is the end of time coming by?

At the thought of death I hide my cry.

A Deathly Feel

At times like this, it's hard to find something to write,
When death suddenly approaches causing you fright,
It happens so blindly and forever so quick,
How long left, has our heart got to tick.

Numbness lives, deep inside my head,
Words can't explain what I feel for the dead,
Families devastated are lonely left behind,
The rules of life are so unfairly, unkind.

The good Lord has taken many, but for what reason,
On Earth, my home, there's so much death this season,
Fire and flood have come at Mother Nature's call,
Unfortunate accidents, caused others to fall.

Death hits hard, when it's close to home,
Shock silences speech, to that of a gnome,
So still is the mind in the time that we grieve,
Stuck in a state that is not easy to leave.

It is never the same, but life must go on,

With their faces absent, memories last long,

For respect, flowers scent, blow through the air,

Wooden crosses erected, show who died there.

The pain lessens slowly, as each day goes by,

For the ones we loved, there's always a cry,

They'd want you to make the most of your time,

So awake from the dream and see the sent sign.

There is life after death, reincarnation is true,

Only when the time's right, the Lord will take you,

It can be sooner than later, so cherish each day,

Appreciate your life and the bed where you lay.

Every day the eyes open has to be great,

Achieve all to be achieved before it's too late,

Tomorrow can bring the most unexpected fall,

Who knows when the good Lord will call?

Bedtime

When the light goes out
And darkness unfolds,
Light a candle to find
That it's too hot to hold.

Sedated in bed dreaming
With eyes open wide,
Watching wax melt
And drip down the side.

In a flame lit room
I sense an empty space,
Right beside where I lay
There is a special place.

The emptiness I feel
I'm really beginning to hate,
I ask myself inside my head
Where is my soul mate?

The candle still burns
While the mind is still dreaming,
With eyes wide open
The shadows are still flickering.

Meditated thoughts are so silent
Setting the mind free,
Making one wonder
Who'll be the one that lays beside me.

For my healing fingers need
A spine to walk up and down,
While the thumb sensates
Spinning itself round and round.

To the rhythm of the flame
That is swaying in the breeze,
The hand will move freely
Causing any pain to ease.

A struggling flame is trying
To keep itself alight,
Empty arms are hoping
For someone to hold tight.

Into melted wax, fighting
The fire finally dies,
So I roll over wishing that
I could look into her eyes.

Then in the darkest hour
From dreams I awake,
I am realising after
The deep breath that I take.

That the mind is so lonely
Inside these four walls,
So the ears are always listening
For when the angel calls.

Chapter Four

Emotions, From Deep within a Man

Highly present in the midst of an emotional hailstorm
So many variables generating unnameable feelings,
Strangers become friends in so little time
Friends become stronger growing together this life,
Sincerity offered first hand, for no need required
The joy found in this realisation, infinitely priceless

Heart of Pain

Rip out my heart
Drag it across the floor,
Stain blood with dirt
Make it more sore.

Leave it there
Trashed in pain,
Kick it, flog it
Wash it down the drain.

I don't need it
But you do,
All it ever gave
Was just true.

Now it is gone
Blood soaks clothes,
And from my chest
Red liquid flows.

Tasting this blood
Makes me truly thrive,
To let me know
That I am still alive.

Grey

Walls grey stand tall,
Deathly grey, enormous fall,
Man's creation, rape,
Earth, in pieces take.

Our backyard a grave,
Nothing at all we save,
Deeper daily for gold,
On my soul there is a hold.

Can't shake it, it stays,
Conditioned to it, mind plays,
Need to escape, now,
Tried everything, how?

Nothing works only me,
Blinded by figure, can't see,
Adding up, I only come down,
Permanent becomes the frown.

Straining, struggling, fighting,
My energy, myself I'm biting,
Scaring the skull I own,
Silent is the pain I moan.

Wanting to give in, the end,
Death, is it a good friend?
All problems, would they cease
If added to the list of deceased?

So grey the colour of death,
I breathe it every breath,
Choking lungs, I don't want to die,
Happiness, can I buy?

No, it must be found,
Inside, silent I think it sounds,
All answers I seem to know,
But to that place, why can't I go?

Men

A room of men
In pain, hurting
Looking for more,
Searching life
Real men talking
Sharing their hearts
No shame, lots of guilt
Anger, raging.

With each other they confide
Living a virtue
Honesty, like not before
Stories unfold
The pain groans,
Layers upon layers
Are slowly torn back
Till there, it is seen.

The rawness, cut so deep
It hurts, oh it hurts,
Thresholds exceeded
It is alive,
Not even the deepest gash
Oozing excruciating amounts of blood
Putting one on death's bed
Could compare to this pain.

I see their eyes
I see their thirst
I see their change
Bit by bit, slowly
Every meeting of these men
A subtle shift is happening,
Their minds are opening
Along with their hearts.

To the source of life
Men, tough like steel
Are allowing themselves
To be touched by its powers above,
Men, real men in a room
Men who can say they have lived life
Tough men, strong men
Men that are getting stronger.

Men surrendering to the conditioning
Are opening their hearts to the way,
Men begin to live the mystery,
The mystery of life
As they look for more,
I see the ending near
I see the beginning ahead
Deep inside, I see.

Men look, finding
The infinite gold within oneself,
Men of this world
Brought together for reason,
Growing, thriving
As the old is buried
And the new is born,
What a sight.

Men of this world
Just being men of this world,
Loving, caring
Gentle, honest
And most of all
Serving within the great mystery itself
And allowing themselves
To just be done.

Where I Sit

Am I meant to be here
In this place that I sit?
At this very point in time
Is it right, is this it?

The vibe tells me no
It's just a mere step,
To get to somewhere greater
Where love can be kept.

Anxious to get there
The body fills with stress,
Locked away in isolation
Trying to clean the mess.

I really thought this chosen road
Was going to be the right,
Conflicting voices speak
One says dark, one says light.

Both I know are right
Without one, the other can't exist,
In the darkest hour
Light can kill the mist.

Just a little is required
To regain a pinch of hope,
But through this mere step
How much longer can I cope?

Life is being sucked
From my soul it is taking,
Being run into the ground
When it is love, I could be making.

For myself and someone else
True, it will be found,
Cannot come this far
To fall into silent sound.

My mind makes a future
Out of ego, full of dreams,
Loud, it wants to live
Get me there, the voices scream.

But will it make any difference
When I get to that point in time?
Why can't it be here and now
That an angel sends a sign?

From underneath the halo
She'll be flying free,
Gowned in a white satin dress
Her wings I want to see.

Hovering high above me
A whisper will be enough,
To ease this troubled mind
From getting dragged through the rough.

Hurting nearly bleeding
Close is many a tear,
Building up like a storm
Enough to fill a weir.

Letting it all flow freely
Makes the emotion a friend,
Conquering this long lost portal
There's no limit to the end.

Having not given into the vibe

That amplifies the feeling no,

A lonely soul sees an angel

Whispering these words slow.

You are meant to be here

In this place that you sit,

At this very point in time

It is right, this is it.

Anger

Trying to deal with anger
This situation doesn't help,
A hand of torment
Is what has been dealt.

The road is badly broken
So torture it comes slow,
When one wound heals
They fire from their bow.

Arrows are sharply shot
Accurate, they don't miss,
But till they hit my heart
I'll just blow another kiss.

And with that a smile too
It hurts even more,
Though my anger it is raging
Ready, it is to pour.

Holding back, breathing
Dissolving the emotion,
Where's the white witch?
With the curing potion.

I need to see her
Or an explosion will erupt,
My soul with powerful magic
I will let her corrupt.

No signs she has surfaced
It is a lonely battle,
From a cage within
My anger, vicious, rattles.

It's a repetitious wave
Crashing to rebuild,
Sentenced are many others
That from it has killed.

I know I won't follow
But I know I receive,
Fighting it, struggling
I just want it to leave.

Bit by bit, chipping
I need to make a change,
The life situation present
Is so familiar it is strange.

Knowing what is needed
To escape this torment,
Along with the next kiss
An arrow will be sent.

Hitting its target hard
Love it was sent to find,
Easing all the anger
That has built inside my mind.

From that moment on
All is turned around,
To accept oneself
As a purpose is found.

The road badly broken
Then starts to mend,
Through the tunnel long
There's a light at the end.

Though the battle fought
Is not over yet,
More guidance is required
From witch white, I can get.

When the time is right
I know she'll present,
In darker times before
Her ear she has lent.

So until that time comes
In myself I must look,
To distinguish what chapter
I am in this book.

Towards the end of another
Reflecting I realise,
So much has been witnessed
From behind these two eyes.

Making a self out of mind
That person I'll forget,
To move forward directly
Not to any regret.

The past is the past

And it always will be,

So alive in the now

My anger is set free.

Mine

Torn into two
Shred,
Weighted by lead
Dead.

Pain so much
Grows,
Life's little seeds
Unsow.

Looking so down
Frown,
Darkened ground
Bound.

Seen it before
Whore,
Different law
Judge more.

Careless evil witch
Stitched,
To curse my soul
Bitch.

Hate, hate, hate
Hate,
Little too late
Fate.

Little lost boy
Costs,
Never could cost
Cover loss.

Aw, my blood
Mine,
Will kill
Mine.

Where is my Child

Where is my child
Where does he hide?
Nothing at all but pain
I feel inside.

Shut off from existence
No time to play,
Life is so narrowed
Still trapped today.

I can't find love
All I feel is hate,
Stuck in this rut
I want out of this state.

I look for answers
But I just don't know,
Raw is this deal
Through it I go.

Every step so important
I will come out,
It takes pure strength
To win this bout.

So as the journey goes on
Something has died,
As I ask, where is my child
Where does he hide?

Dark Hole

I've been rejected
I've been abandoned
I've been abused,
Like a piece of trash
At times it feels like
I have been used.

I've felt scared
I've felt sad
I have felt as if I am all alone,
With nowhere else
But inside myself
I have buried this painful moan.

I have run
I have hid
But now, I don't know where to go,
A little child
With a broken heart
Unnurtured, this I do know.

So much pain

Answers come

But how to soothe this soul?

Down so deep

It's dark and black

You don't want this darkened hole.

My Little Boy

Daddy has some problems
That you are unaware,
But this doesn't mean
That Daddy doesn't care.

All that has happened
For nothing you're to blame,
You just need to know
That Daddy loves you all the same.

With these arms around you
Please cry away your tears,
It is best you are here now
You have nothing more to fear.

In time to come you'll see
Perfect, every day,
You just need to know
It's now time for you to play.

It's okay my little boy, my little boy
Come, tell me what they've done,
It's okay my little boy, my little boy
I feel your pain, deep inside.

It's okay my little boy, my little boy
I know you're sad, very sad,
It's okay my little boy, my little boy
If you need to cry, then cry.

I Hold You

I feel you there lonely one
Scared of the she boss,
With arms tight, I hold you
Fearful of more loss.

Just know I am here
Together, we'll make it through,
Feeling that deep pain
Ingrained, another path now new.

Whatever will unfold
In the days up ahead,
Close by my side you'll be
As we hear the answers said.

Just know God is good
Together we'll make it through,
Once he has waved his hand
The path will show us what to do.

Believe my boy have faith,
Safe I will keep you kept,
No matter where we go
To the side you won't be swept.

Just know I am here,
Together we'll make it through,
Nurturing you with Grandma's arms
So damn tight and close, I hold you.

Deep

Deep, oh so deep
It sits below the heart,
Stirring, brewing
Rumbling, groaning
What is it I ask?
It wants to rise
It confuses thought
Frustrating, it won't go away.

On the verge of anger
I watch it
I feel it,
My higher self analyses
Finding only one answer
Rejection,
Conditioned from childhood
Always expecting the worse.

How to break the cycle

I do not know,

So aware, under control

But still being the addiction,

Looking outside for fulfilment

Looking outside for love,

Wanting someone so dearly

To give attention.

When it is there

I feel so good

When it is not

This feeling sits and brews,

So much on board

Consumed by a battle

Energy is low, time to give in,

Give it all away.

I'm losing care

Not for life

But just the things you find self in,

Time to reassess

Time to search for faith

So little do I find

How can I believe

This moment is perfect?

All I feel is pain
Sitting deep within it I stay
Putting my full attention on it
I watch,
There's no way out
Except through it
So as I go further into it, I see
Nothing really matters.

There is no wrong or right,
Expectations lead to disaster
Though disaster is only a perception –
One created by the mind,
Just let this all be
And in divine order
All will be put into place
Rightfully it will be placed.

There it is, right there
The wisdom within
Connected to the source
Allowing life to flow freely,
With great pride
I can say
I have risen above
To find stillness, deep inside.

Angry, Hurt, Faith

The fist is clenched
The jaw shut solid
Teeth grind
Backward and forward
An angry rage burns silent
The heart trampled
Amplifies this hurting pain
Throbbing after the initial shock.

Identifying with thought
Concerns heightened
Decisions questioned, is this right?
The intensity bearable though continuous
A process in place, just let me be in it
I will come out, I won't fall
Though I feel like starting a fucking war
New patterns are stronger.

All I can do is love, love, love
No one's to blame
Two hurt humans, mistaken, mislead
All that has happened, perfect,
All for the higher good
Though the pain is no less,
Feels like I'm losing my best friend
When all I want to do is hold her tight.

Reality, my son
It's not going to happen
Love and let go, be strong
The timing just isn't right,
Walk away now
Continue the rebuild of life
It's under construction
The tunnel ahead, you must walk alone.

Clarity in voices will be heard
And the knowing is yours to be had,
Listen my precious one
Rebuild your faith
Walk this new path
The path known as your life,
Success is to be had
All you have to do is believe in yourself.

There it is
Right in the palm of your hand,
Look no further your talent prevails,
A child of God
One of a kind of many perfect creations
Blessed and protected by angels of light,
Sleep now my son
Let peace rest upon your being.

Give thanks to share in the suffering
That our world is drowning in
At this present point in time,
To receive the highs of life
All at some point in time
Must visit the fires of trials,
Be still and know
This moment is meant to be.

Don't Back Down

When deep down inside
You know you are right,
Stand by the belief
From your soul fight.

Rise to a height
Never back down,
Take the whole lot
All the way to town.

Direct the sentence
So it is heard,
To the universe
Send by a bird.

All will hear
That lives and breathes,
No matter how minor
Your purpose you need.

No one nothing
Your purpose, your own,
Cuts into wounds deep
Before the groan.

Standing proud
Results appear,
Eye to eye
Authority stays clear.

Beaten by strength
Built from within,
Squirming and squawking
It was no sin.

Just a belief
In that I believed,
From the soul deep
I've come to succeed.

Mind

My mind is silent
Sitting still,
Free of thought
If any kill.

The higher self
Watches down,
Angers absent
Without a frown.

Lifted lighter
Life is great,
Slowly disposed
Mental hate.

Looking high
Moon in halves,
Universe revolves
Mother Nature laughs.

Nothing worries
In time unfair,
Deep inside
Tired I care.

Strange is this
No voices speak,
Rhyming words
I only seek.

In control
Peace I find,
For I'm free
Of my mind.

On Edge

Why am I here
In this state of mind?
My purpose in life
I need to find.

Can't take much more
Of solitary confinement,
Too much time alone
Has now been spent.

I want to daze in a park
Sitting still and free,
Observing the people
Who walk pass me.

Sick of society
And the battle that's fought,
How many lessons?
Need to be taught.

Too many it seems
As I fight on,
Close to surrender
But I am strong.

That's the problem
I can't give in,
To me that seems
Like an evil sin.

To whom to talk?
When no one's around,
Repetitious thoughts
Are the only sound.

Accept this moment
For it I chose,
Presence comes forward
As unconsciousness goes.

True Colours

Seeing true colours
Theirs, they are real,
Disgusts my being
Attempting to heal.

Main focus, life
They can't defeat,
Conditioned to fight
Their colours I beat.

Tearing shreds
Nowhere they've been,
Practised, no mind
Pathway is clean.

Situation obstructed
Not primary source,
Keep colours out
With positive force.

Seeing true colours
Theirs, they are real,
My worries lesson
Goodness I feel.

Through their evil
Black coloured approached,
The myself, I am
Creatively coached.

Laughing like Buddha
Their colours aren't mine,
Never drawn near
Life's on incline.

Growing deeply enlightened
They're blinded by light,
Keeping their colours
True, I win fight.

I am Worth

Every second's like a minute
Every minute's like an hour,
Tonight the clock stands still
Draining my vital power.

Sucking life from inside
All I need is sleep,
But the master cracks the whip
To rape the Earth from deep.

Locked in a vicious cycle
A slave is all you are,
Bottled up inside tight
Then the lid closes on the jar.

Chains are locked around you
You may as well been thrown to sea,
But then it'd be a waste
So you're tortured with the key.

One day I'll break the glass
And get it in my hands,
To show the whole wide world
Who is in control of my man.

The time's not quite right
So for the ride I go along,
Knowing that within myself
That I am growing strong.

Deep beneath the surface
My plan has started to grow,
Sprouted roots are thriving
Starting short and widening slow.

Through times tough, they do dig
Binding to the Earth,
Fighting for survival
My own life I know I'm worth.

My Enemy or Myself

Round and round in circles
Heavy thoughts flow,
Trying to find an answer
Negativity says no.

No answer can one find
Let the mechanics be,
To escape this vicious torture
Of mind, I want to be set free.

Nowhere does it go
One thing just leads to the next,
Draining all the goodness
Is this thought driven text.

I tell you right now
All I want is out,
Why am I addicted?
All of it I doubt.

Endless mind dysfunction
Is driving me insane,
Amplified thought filled patterns
Create emotional pain.

Not much more can I take
Of this teeth grinding chatter,
The worse thing of all
Is I know it doesn't matter.

But I do know it's there
Manifesting deep inside,
Surrendering to life's walk
No one can hurt my pride.

Though they have been tearing
My spirit's been attacked,
All the odds are against me
And high I see them stacked.

So I just keep fighting
My enemy and myself,
Who will kill me first?
My enemy or myself.

At the Bottom

In a dark place, life
Down in the dregs of the barrel
Washing side to side
Arms tied, invisible rope
Can't see any light
Walls, caving in
Drowning, can't breathe
Being taken under.

Fighting to survive
Please help, someone
Please, I want to live
No more darkness
Take it away, shine a light
Bright, please God
Help, take my hand
Pull me out.

Give me hope, I need it
Now, can't wait longer
I'm dying inside,
This darkness kills
Never before been this low
Time, time to rise
Where's my guide?
Spoken about, never seen.

Is the spirit real?
Show me a sign
Confusion absorbed
Want to believe
Mind created myths
Create dysfunction
Shining darkness
All over the world.

Our species insane
Me included
Trapped in darkness
Still no light
Life, can't get any darker
This I hope
I really hope
God, I live with hope.

Chapter Five

Walking in the Spirit

Eyes connect beautifully
Left to left, right to right
Hearts speak truthfully
Letting in the light

Light Attracts Light

So many people breathing
A vibe rather strange,
Set in their culture
Nobody wants change.

Pushing dark aside
Light attracts light,
Creating positivity
No need to fight.

Energy connects
As ideas share,
For one another
We all do care.

In a circle now
Grounded to Earth,
A place is found
Where you are worth.

Setting yourself free
Out of control,
In the right spot
Now is your soul.

Blowing in the wind
With those alike,
Being drawn together
Saving the psych.

Here now to stay
After finding feet,
Far away from darkness
Never again to meet.

This vibe's rewarding
The winner of the fight,
Defeating depths of darkness
As light attracts light.

The God of Oneness

Being in this world
Let us all see the same,
And feel the peace of life
Without a labelled name.

We all breathe the air
On this Earth today,
Created by our Father
Look within to find the way.

Beyond stars the boundary extends
But inside we find the gold,
Worth more than any form
Life, value it does hold.

Nothing can ever explain
The existence of our race,
Conditioned mind-set patterns
Fade to explore grace.

The God of oneness
Is knocking at our door,
Creating wonders
To fill our internal store.

The Great Spirit flows
On our Earth,
After death
There is birth.

New life lives
We're born again,
Free in spirit
No more pain.

Let Me Know the Way

I look to the heavens
That have set this path before me,
Knowing that up there high
The angels have the answers.

Praying to God I ask
Please just let me know the way,
And guide me to fulfil my dreams
The one's I see almost every day.

I don't ask for much
For my dreams are small, simple things,
Desires that aren't necessary
As I know I am complete.

My dreams consist of not
Having to live in any more of this pain,
Please remove it from every cell in my body
And inject life into every vein.

With life I ask for abundance

Abundance of your pure, unconditional love,

Free flowing like a wild river

Not enough of it have I received.

But to you I plead

As I want to shelter safely, in your eternal place,

And find the angel of my dreams

God, please show me the beauty of her face.

I Know

I know you heard my cry

From way above

High in your place,

I know you answered my call

To open a new chapter

Full of your amazing grace.

I just want to say thank you

My gratitude goes out

From way deep within,

I just want to say thank you

For the forgiveness you have given

From my many sin.

I do ask for more

As I need patience

To fulfil my destiny,

I do ask for more

As I seek the face

Of the one meant for me.

So, so beautiful
I marvel at the wonders
Of which you create,
So, so beautiful
Every intricate little feature
Of my soul mate.

I know you heard my cry
From way above
High in your place,
I know you answered my call
As I feel the blessing
Of your unconditional grace.

Golden Chimes

Bells begin to ring
Golden, chiming, sharp,
Angels fly so free
Softly playing harp.

Drawn to God's noise
His hedge has appeared,
Protection within its walls
To home I've been steered.

From one event to the next
Energy, the driving force,
The Lord's set a path
To find my long lost horse.

Reuniting, the Great Spirit
So holy can't forget,
It's always lived inside
But now it's Jesus I have let.

Inviting him into life
Nothing ever felt so right,
With faith I now pray
Before I sleep at night.

Watchmen's Prayer

The Holy Spirit flows
From my head to my toes,
Flushing out all darkness
It's he I feel, Jesus.

Coming into my spirit
The evilness he clears it,
Feeling him within me
So clearly, it's Christ I see.

I see his blood bleeding
Whilst my heart he is feeding,
It's love, love, love, love
That into my being he does shove.

Filling a space so empty
To every cell so sweetly,
Alive within it's a river
Down my neck I begin to shiver.

Satan's demons can't survive
As the watchmen's prayer revives,
Light keeps flushing darkness
To let me see him, Jesus.

Healing this heart of trouble
With his love I face the rubble,
To stare back at the road's fork
And face the path that I walked.

Bringing forgiveness to evil faces
They can't see they are life wasters,
With the Lord, one day, repent
For the evil sins you have spent.

Like I who have risen from darkness
With him our Lord, Jesus,
In God's plan, all evilness will disappear
When his son, our Lord reappears.

Death to Life

A prisoner locked in chains
Hands behind back walking,
Sergeants standing side by side
Flogging this man if talking.

Punishment received so very harsh
Little children taken away hidden,
To this man, God's son
An event considered forbidden.

So much pain is inflicted
The enemy emotionally flogs,
Holding his head down hard
To choke on deadly smog.

Suffocating, not breathing
His stomach knotted intensively,
The struggle, oh the struggle
Life, dying off immensely.

Wait, a vision, two angels
Flying, speaking, don't fear,
They're bringing someone with them
Jesus it is they've brought here.

Coated in brown drapes
Upon the prisoner his hand is set,
The sergeants transform to angels
After Christ it is they've met.

Freeing this poor victim
From chains he is set free,
Looking into the Lord's eyes
Salvation he can see.

Healing, finally comes
Through revelation of Jesus Christ,
Forgiveness of sins requested
And granted by Jesus Christ.

In his name repentance
A new walk begins today,
Following the Holy Spirit
With Jesus I walk – hurray.

Anointed

Sharing hearts
Nothing sacred,
All revealed
Deepest hatred.

Frustration, oh frustration
No end near,
Listen closely
Hear.

A subtle voice
Breathes life,
Life, life, life
Nothing but life.

His presence comes
Lifting, strengthening,
The feeling, oh the feeling
So overwhelming.

His spirit pours
Endlessly within,
Freeing strongholds
Forgiving sin.

His love, oh his love
There's no greater,
Than the love
Of our creator.

So unconditional
So healing,
So indescribable
This anointed feeling.

Let it Pour

Angels of light swooping down
Bringing life into our heart,
Healing wounds of conditioned past
Removing roots from where it all start.

His hand goes deep, way within
As the angels open the way,
Through memories and experiences
The Lord digs, finding a place to stay.

Knowing he's there with angels in force
Heavy pain lifts to dissolve in light,
Praying for forgiveness of sins
The Lord I see dead centre in sight.

Nodding his head, talking to me
I hear him say, "I forgive you my son,
But first repent and then together we'll walk
For you know what wrong you have done".

Breathing deep the Lord's light shines
Making a personal promise, I feel change,
With his loving nature blessed upon my soul
My being, every cell feels rather strange.

Everything is alive, surrounded by light
Defined are all of his creations,
In the presence of God, so great
I find Jesus one of my relations.

Like a brother to the same father
By his spirit so holy I'm now lead,
Walking with him and many angels
My old self is buried dead.

Gone away to be forgotten
Not to live on this Earth any more,
Darkened voids are flushed with light
So let the Holy Spirit pour.

In the Fire

I have seen the fire
Burning the most purest light,
Way above in heaven
It was stoked at great height.

Down it came so close
I could reach out and touch,
The man that lived inside
That man who loves so much.

Bowing down to worship
Both hands out in front raised,
Surrounded by so many angels
Our Lord Jesus Christ is praised.

Coming with the fire's heat
The Holy Spirit brings a tune,
So heavenly it hums along
At church, in a tent, under the moon.

So blessed in our Father's presence
The fire burns as angel's dance,
Lifting, building and cheering
Our Lord comes to make a stance.

Taking away pain and curing addictions
The flames heal the deepest hurt,
Our united Christian family
Kneels down to pray in God's dirt.

Having every prayer answered
Faith rebuilds to the highest degree,
Within the vision of the fire
Many eagles are soaring free.

Like us little human people
Each bird plays their special part,
Knowing they belong to the creator
The man to whom I gave my heart.

Right Now

The presence is here
Of God right now,
Seeds in hand's palm
Rich soil to plough.

A crop in time
No time, tick slow,
From Earth's heaven
Eyes, watch, grow.

Through seasons of flood
Fire or drought,
His plan up above
Will sort it all out.

Believe with faith
And at harvest you'll see,
Much to reap
For both you and me.

So now before you eat
Have a thought of the cost,
That Jesus our Lord paid
When nailed to the cross.

He died for our sins
To be raised from the dead,
So praise the Lord
During prayer before bed.

Believe

Time, so precious
Every minute, every day
More is required
Away from slavery,
It hurts
Wasting one
Into extinction
Endangered is my soul.

A master rules
Telling mind to stay
But one higher
Sees more,
An escape to survive
With spirit ruling
The path to walk
Is bright.

Full of dreams
Instigated
Inside deep
Beyond thought,
Within beliefs
Of something Great
So Great
It lives in all.

Not recognised by some
But by many it is,
The ruler, it is you
See the light
It's shining, guiding to a place
Greater, where love for yourself
Walks free alongside
The love of others.

Together, as one, connected
In a circle that evolves
Life, lives under stars
Within the universe,
Our galaxy is so large
Much can't been seen
Leaving imagination open
Running wild with images.

Other life
With love, must exist
Somewhere, out there
In the unknown
Where?
Fortune lives on Earth
But time's so precious
It can't last forever.

Free yourself
From what you're not
Walk your path
The spirit provides
And in return, just believe
It is yours
Only yours
Take it.

Now's your chance
Be free from the slave
Release the inner genius
Conform to your desires
Open are the doors
You are the master
This is your life
Believe.

New Horizons

Sitting, watching
This moment arises
Watching, silently
Our sun slowly setting,
Light now dimming
The sky changes
Planets, stars
Shine in darkness.

Freedom, peace
Found in stillness
Heart's desire
Spirit is willing,
Fleshy works
Creates conflict
Listening deeply
Cells are working.

Confusion, chaos
Mind is thinking
Pleasure, pain
Always self-inflicted
Eternal love
A gift of grace
Times changing
Chapter closing.

Lessons learnt
Embrace the past
Without darkness
Light cannot shine,
Lighting candles
Dreams come slowly
Dying quickly
Pursuing harshly.

Walking newly
The old now buried
Covered red
In the blood of Christ
Resistance lives
Though words speak different
Easily say
"This creation's new".

Old, so much
Highly aware
Caution, care
Can't change a thing
Except the person
That now you'll be –
Perspective changed
Life transitioned.

Rebuild, reform
Out of the valley
Head, high
Foundation is set,
Succeed, success
To the top rising
Striving, arriving
At the light.

Grabbing intensely
Not to let go
Complete moment
It won't come again
Sacred memories
Have just been witnessed
Horizons
Now new.

Free

Free to make choices

What choices to make?

A world full of opportunity

The road forks so much,

Side streets serve a purpose

Each one alight

Never any wrong

Only the highest purpose is served.

At this moment

So present in time

Everything is put to the side,

To dwell in stillness

No step, no choice

Nothing is made

Sitting in peace

Knowing things will change.

Timing, crucial
Just let it all be
No resistance
Pure acceptance
This too will pass,
Loneliness
The world is out there
For one's taking.

Every step, even the still ones
Have to be taken
Without the stops,
There is no start
Believe, and just be done
By the spirit, that created all
The Great Spirit
The one that calls.

Chapter Six

The Ones Held Closest to Heart

This very moment so many stars fill the sky
Creation, stillness, unexplainable, why?
Twinkling, sparkling, the universe talks to me
Constellations, stories, love, it is so free,
Connected, one, in the presence of a Spirit Great
Peace, knowing, this moment is fate
Realisation a powerful hand wrote this moment true
This very moment all I can do is think of you

Smile Your Smile

Weeping a tear
I wipe it away,
But for a reason
In my heart you stay.

The path of the past
Hard to forget,
But not to see you again
Is something I'd regret.

Pain and hurt linger
Living deep inside,
But memories of you
Have never ever died.

You are my Sister
That you'll always be,
So smile your smile
And set your spirit free.

The time is coming
The Greater Spirit lives,
Watching over our lives
There's so much it gives.

To reunite again
The flame will burn,
From painful mistakes
We all will learn.

Peace we will find
As the future unfolds,
Deep in my heart
It is love that I hold.

You are my Sister
You will always be,
So smile your smile
Right beside me.

Mother

She was the one
To carry me to Earth,
Always to be there
From the day of my birth.

My Mother, my provider
Gave love from the start,
From deep inside
Deep in her heart.

Still to this day
I feel her love,
No matter where I am
She looks down from above.

And my love for her too
It is so dear,
Nothing could replace
The love I hold here.

Here in my heart
A space she fills,
So special it is
And it always will.

The distance between
Hurts like hell,
Memories of our time
In my thoughts dwell.

With motherly love
You made me this man,
And In return
I made you a Gran.

Nothing, no one
Can show love the same,
She is my Mother
And Mum is her name.

*The two most beautiful ladies that have greatly influenced my life,
my Mother Chris and Grandmother Joyce.*

*Embracing a special moment of love with our Grandmother Joyce,
From left to right, Tim, cousins Clare and Michael, my little sister Jamie.*

*The poem on the following page I recited at my Grandmother's funeral,
it was composed the night before.*

Granny's Poem

I can nearly remember back
To the day that I was born,
Kicking the footy
On Granny's Avenell Street lawn.

Sometimes Clare and Mick
Would come to stay,
And you know what
It was Uno we played.

Granny showed me
The eyes of the cat,
But I never let her know
I hit Mick on his head with a bat.

She'd always spread butter
Thick with her knife,
Bert was so lucky
To have Nugget for his wife.

Granny used to have
A big jarful of lollies,
And when she went shopping in the rain
She'd always have a brollie.

Another thing I know
Is when walking up the street,
Granny, you'd always drop
Your bloody handkerchief.

The Grandchildren you loved
Were Clare and Mick, Amy and Tim,
Then there was Jamie
Who we found in the bin.

We all dearly loved
The way you were,
The humming you hummed
Was natural, like a cat that purred.

Granny always lent me money
When I needed smokes,
Or to go to the pub
To have a drink with the blokes.

She was always there
When I needed a bed,
And I'd never leave her home
Without being well fed.

I don't know what to do
Now I am without you,
Because I already know
That I already miss you.

There's not much else
That I can really say,
'Granny' Rest in Peace in Heaven
In the light of day.

*Smiling her smile and as beautiful as her Grandmother,
my sister Amy with her son Lachlan and Grandmother Joyce.*

My favourite photo of all time, me and my Grandmother Joyce.

12 Years On

I feel your presence, great
In my life, always, every day,
From that eternal place
Right beside me you've come to stay.

Dwelling in thought, deeply
Tears run freely, memories true,
Reflecting my pain filled life
Unconditionally, there was you.

Arms always open, so warm
My head would sink into your chest,
A heart of love, so pure
Granny, you were the God damn best.

Inside me, nothing, no one
Will ever come to replace,
This spot I've deep in my heart
Painted bright is your face.

I will never forget our time
Though dearly I do miss,
Every detail of your being
Especially the Grandma's kiss.

Now far from your place, high above
My needs you continue to serve,
Still helping a hurt little boy
Providing the nurturing he does deserve.

So grateful of your presence
I know you'll never leave,
With your hand still upon mine
Your love I always receive.

So now as I lay down my pen
And sink my head into your chest,
I feel your heart of love, so pure
Granny, you were the God damn best.

9 780099 413307